The Films of

MARLON BRANDO

Heroes of the Movies – Marlon Brando

Library of Congress Cataloging in Publication Data

Braithwaite, Bruce.
The films of Marlon Brando.

1. Brando, Marlon. I. Title.
PN2287.B683B7 1982 791.43′028′0924 [B] 82-12888
ISBN 0-8253-0108-4 (Beaufort Books)

Published in the United States by Beaufort Books, Inc.,
New York, and The Confucian Press, Inc.
Publishing simultaneously in Canada by
General Publishing Co. Limited

Printed in the U.S.A.   First Edition
10 9 8 7 6 5 4 3 2 1

The Films of
MARLON
BRANDO

Bruce Braithwaite

THE CONFUCIAN PRESS, INC.

•

BEAUFORT BOOKS, INC.

New York/Toronto

Marlon Brando was born in Omaha, Nebraska on April 3, 1924, the third child and only son of Marlon Brando Snr and Dorothy Pennebaker. The family name was originally spelt Brandeau and the family is of French extraction, explaining perhaps Marlon's deep and abiding love of Paris. Those who knew him well say there was a great deal of Marlon's childhood and father-son relationship revealed in the tortuous monologues in *Last Tango in Paris*. Some say it was without doubt his most personal film. But whatever the truth of that may be, the childhood of the man who was to become one of the most influential actors of the twentieth century was a fairly typical middle-class one. Brando's mother had a great enthusiasm for acting; although she never became an actress herself, she inspired in her children a love of creative things. Marlon idolised her and never forgave his father for the sporadic unhappiness which the children witnessed was her lot. As an adult, Brando said of his father: "He was indifferent to me; nothing I could do interested him or pleased him." Although in later life he and his father reached a more placid understanding, old hurts never healed and Marlon was distraught when his father re-married after his mother's death. At one time he was furious to discover that his father had opened a letter addressed to "Marlon Brando" and, finding it to be a letter to his son, sent it on to him with a note of apology. Marlon demanded that his father change his name only to be told, "It's my name too and I've had it for thirty-five years longer than you have."

When Marlon Jnr was six, the family began their travels — first to Illinois, then California, then back to Illinois. He was a wilful child. Even as a small boy he was forever acting out scenes, testing how quickly he could eat, holding his breath for the longest possible time. He was insecure and competitive and hated being regimented. He loathed school although he excelled at athletics. Throughout his school life he rebelled against the authority of the teachers and consequently was not the most popular pupil. Eventually his father decided that what he needed was some military discipline, so Marlon was despatched to the Shattuck Academy in Minnesota, which his father had attended. He was fifteen. There are many different versions about what happened while he was there (Brando, in the rare interviews he does give, tends to vary the story according to his mood) but the end result was that he was expelled a few weeks before graduating.

"I hated it every day I was there. The authorities annoyed me. I had to show respect to those for whom I had no respect. I also hated clocks. I love the kind of life where time doesn't matter, but the bell at the Academy chimed every quarter hour and I loathed it. One night I climbed to the top of the tower and worked the clapper loose. Then I buried it in the ground." The sound of the clapper was replaced by boy buglers – which was even worse.

Marlon drifted following his expulsion. He debated becoming a minister of the church, he worked briefly for a constructor, digging ditches and laying tiles. The open air work appealed to him but the job was tedious in the extreme. Brando's older sisters were both in New York – Frances was studying art and Jocelyn was already acting. He hitch-hiked to New York and moved in with Frances. His possessions were few – a tom-tom, a recorder, a small red piano, one suit and a collection of T-shirts and blue jeans. Later it would become a uniform, copied strenuously by a generation. But Brando was the first.

He enrolled at the Dramatic Workshop of the New School for Social Research. An actress recalled the impact he made on the class: "He was the most desirable, sensual young guy I ever saw. He had animal magnetism that grabbed you and a beautiful, sensitive face. He could be a charmer: he had star quality and we all knew it."

In student productions, Marlon began to be noticed by critics. At this time he began his association with acting coach Stella Adler and the Actors' Studio. "I taught him nothing," she said later. "I opened up possibilities of thinking, feeling, experiencing. I opened those doors and he walked right through. He never needed me after that. He lived the life of an actor twenty-four hours a day. If he is talking to you he will absorb everything about you – your smile, the way your teeth grow. His style is the perfect marriage of intuition and intelligence."

Stella Adler was confident when she predicted that very soon Marlon would be the best actor in the American theatre. She did not have long to wait. At twenty, he made his Broadway debut in "I Remember Mama", a debut that was noted favourably by the critics. Brando improvised his biography for the programme notes with each subsequent play. His place of birth varied from Calcutta (where, so the fiction told, his father was doing geological research), to Rangoon, Bombay or Bangkok. "Why shouldn't I have a different place

Opposite: with Kim Stanley in A Streetcar Named Desire

for my birth in every theatre programme if I feel like it? What difference does it make?" But although the young Brando had scant regard for this kind of social nicety, and was constantly playing practical jokes on people (something he has done throughout his career, although he hates to be at the receiving end), he was still searching for answers. He enrolled for courses in psychology, the history of art, conversational French, and graphology.

His behaviour covered the whole spectrum from rational to irrational. He was soon to become a superstar and there are some who say that he always felt guilty about the lack of struggle, that he believes acting is an unworthy profession for a grown man. He has always refused to analyse too deeply the way he acts — believing, possibly, that too much investigation negates both the effect of what he does and puts his very ability at risk.

Under the tuition of Elia Kazan (a seminal influence on Brando's acting career) Brando directed a student production of "Hedda Gabler". The Broadway production of "Truckline Cafe" in 1946 brought Marlon once again into the star orbit and he went on to do "Candida" and "The Eagle Has Two Heads" with Tallulah Bankhead. There was a severe personality clash. "He drove me to distraction," said Miss Bankhead. "She didn't like me," said Brando. He left the production and spent a year travelling around, experiencing that more potent force — life.

Being a restless soul, he kept moving from one small, uncomfortable apartment to another and subsequent tenants had to pin a note to their front door saying, "Marlon doesn't live here any more," to stem the flow of girlfriends in search of Brando.

Marlon had always been careless with money: when he had it, he spent it, gave it away or left it around. His income was growing but his ability to handle it was nil. He and his father started a company to invest Marlon's earnings. It was called the Marsdo (Marlon's dough) Holding Company. The turning point in his life was the Broadway production of "A Streetcar Named Desire". Tennessee Williams met Brando and was impressed by him. When John Garfield, then at the height of his career, turned down the role of Stanley Kowalski, because he felt that it was overshadowed by Blanche, Tennessee Williams and Elia Kazan cast Brando.

It was this play that made him the hero of New York and the most sought-after of young actors. It was also the play that

Opposite: as Napoleon Bonaparte in Desiree

lost Brando to the movies because, when he left Broadway for Hollywood, he never returned. "It was awful and it was sublime. Only once in a generation do you see such a thing in the theatre," was one critical response to Brando's performance in "A Streetcar Named Desire". His parents arrived in New York for the opening night and his friends were amused to see their wild companion become a model son − if only for a while. Marlon did not get on with his "Streetcar" leading lady, Jessica Tandy, but he managed quite well with virtually every other lady in town.

"It took me a long time before I was aware that I was a big success. I was so absorbed in myself, my own problems, I never looked around or took account. I used to walk in New York late at night and never see anything. I was never sure about acting, whether that was what I really wanted to do. I'm still not. Then one night, after 'Streetcar' had been running a couple of months, I began to hear this roar. It was like I'd been asleep and I woke up here sitting on a pile of candy."

He is a complex man. He makes sublime acting look easy, and life look hard. Elia Kazan, sensing his insecurities, suggested Marlon try analysis, which he did, and which he claims helped him. "I was afraid of analysis at first. Afraid it might destroy the impulses that made me creative, an artist. A sensitive person receives fifty impressions where somebody else may only get seven. Sensitive people are so vulnerable, they're so easily brutalised and hurt just because they *are* sensitive. The more sensitive you are, the more certain you are to be brutalised, to develop scabs. Never evolve. Never allow yourself to feel anything because you feel too much."

Hollywood was ready for Marlon Brando − ready and waiting. Like tense citizens anticipating the cyclone of which meteorologists have warned, the movie colony had considered Brando's stage reputation, his talent, his tendency to outrage the accepted order. Perhaps they saw a storm brewing, but the financial benefits clearly outweighed the emotional upsets. Several overtures were made to the moody, electric actor who had set alight the New York stage, but independent observers were quite firm in the opinion that it would take a major project, like the film of *A Streetcar Named Desire*, to tempt Brando to the Coast. He had earlier been vocal in his contempt for the product of the Hollywood system, and it is to be noted that not more than a dozen times in a quarter century has the actor been tempted into

Opposite: playing crazy in the farce Bedtime Story

the mainstream. Against the tide: that was the direction Brando invariably went. And when the news leaked out that he had signed for his first film, the only sounds besides the gasps of astonishment were the mouths of jealous producers gaping open. They had promised him the moon and the stars, and this contrary upstart had settled for a very small piece of earth.

The Men was a courageous film made early in the burgeoning career of Stanley Kramer. It was a crusading but commercially poisonous account of a paraplegic's attempts to come to terms with his disability. Brando played Ken, a young soldier whose souvenir of World War II is a sniper's bullet lodged at the base of his spine. The film follows his initial reaction of disbelief at his abrupt paralysis, through broodiness, self-pity and withdrawal to a growing determination to lead as normal a life as possible, go through with his marriage to his sweetheart (Teresa Wright) and try to understand the difficulties that confront a paraplegic's wife. It was a relatively uncompromising film, though a streak of sentimentality somehow filtered through the stern documentary technique. Brando himself was remarkable, subduing completely the charisma and dousing the electricity

Above: in the controversial Last Tango in Paris. Opposite: in Queimada

for which he had become famous. He sunk his whole personality into that of the character, and it came as no surprise to learn later that the actor had in fact spent several weeks among the paraplegics (who appeared as themselves in the film). The humanity in the performance was in the fact that it was so selfless. But sheer intuition and technique proved that the screen had won a rare new talent.

Hollywood was appalled by the superstar from Broadway. Who did he think he was, this ill-mannered, mumbling young man with his grubby T-shirts and tattered jeans, his disgraceful eating habits and incoherent arrogance?

"The only reason I'm here is because I don't yet have the moral strength to turn down the money," was his statement on arriving. But he did show that he was serious about acting. Nevertheless, he certainly wasn't being accepted by the Hollywood gossip queens — Hedda Hopper, Louella Parsons and Sheilah Graham. He had been introduced to Sheilah Graham by his co-star Jessica Tandy in New York and had asked, "Is this your mother?" He referred to Louella Parsons as "the fat one". During an interview with Hedda Hopper he gave "one and a half grunts" in half an hour and when asked if he would like to continue at a later date he said, "Yes," and walked out. But if the gossip columnists —who in those days had enormous power — called him "the slob" and loathed him, fellow actors tended to respect the way he had the courage not to cowtow to the terrible trio. But while other actors admired his willingness to enrage the columnists they were less entranced with the Brando style of acting, the "Method". (Alfred Hitchcock once said, memorably, when asked by a Method actor about the motivation for a scene: "The motivation is your salary.)

The following year Elia Kazan translated his stage production of "A Streetcar Named Desire" on to film. It certainly was not a recreation of a theatrical event although, of necessity, Tennessee Williams' play dictated a certain claustrophobia of action. Vivien Leigh played the gently demented Blanche who brings her daydreams of faded gentility to the drab home of her younger sister, Stella (Kim Hunter), and Stella's brutish husband, Stanley. Thereafter the three are locked in a kind of self-torturing mental combat that is the Williams speciality. Those who have seen Brando's Stanley Kowalski on stage claim that he made many subtle alterations for the film version. Viewing it for the first time, it is a totally compelling and convincing display of animal magnetism:

Opposite: with Sandra Church in The Ugly American

violent, explosive and with a rich texture of underlying sexuality. Many regard it as his finest role.

Marlon Brando became a screen superstar. His torn T-shirt, his aggressive masculinity burned its virile image into the universal consciousness. He was unique and original, but there were many imitators. Brando later admitted that *Streetcar* was his most satisfactory acting experience. From the moody and uncommunicative Kowalski, Brando moved to political ideology (again with Kazan as his mentor) in *Viva Zapata!* John Steinbeck's script looked at the minutiae of the Mexican revolution while dressing its hero in a cloak of legend. Zapata's hands may not have been as bloodless as Brando's, but Kazan brought to his direction all the vigour and action that the material in *Streetcar* necessarily precluded. It was probably this touch of adventure that put the film on the road to success with contemporary audiences. Today it is regarded as a classic though, curiously, keen admirers of Brando do not rate his interpretation of the title role among his better works. In fact he managed astonishingly well to combine legend, political idealism and romantic heroism into one intricate, anguished performance.

By now Brando had a reputation as a specialist in tormented, non-communicative brutes whose hallmark (still perpetuated by the mimics of today) was an inability to enunciate. Hollywood may be keen to hand out labels, but Brando's was (at this point, at any rate) undeserved. It seemed to spring from the characteristics with which Brando had chosen to invest the illiterate Pole, Kowalski, and which were by now being quite widely imitated by fellow graduates of the Stanislavski stable. In any event, the announcement that he was to play Mark Antony in a traditionally classical movie of *Julius Caesar* caught Hollywood off-guard. The casting of Donald Duck in "Macbeth" wouldn't have caused more furore. There was wild conjecture and public ridicule, all silenced when the film appeared and Brando was seen to sit happily in the company of such "classical" actors (one assumes that "classical" is synonymous with "British" in this context) as James Mason and John Gielgud. The presence in the cast of Greer Garson and those denizens of gangster movies, Edmond O'Brien and Louis Calhern, had caused no stir. On reflection, it was quite apposite. This strikingly literate and valid production of *Julius Caesar* was a thinking man's gangster movie, and Brando's reflective Antony no less a rebel than Kowalski.

Opposite: in the Arthur Penn western The Missouri Breaks

But though a bid had been made on his behalf for respectability, Brando's early film career had one more gesture of rebel defiance in it. This was *The Wild One*, a precursor of today's bike movies and a *cause célèbre* in both its country of origin and in Britain, where it remained banned by the vigilant censor until 1968. The film was based on a true incident. A gang of rebel motorcyclists invaded a small American town and terrorised the citizens over the period of a weekend. The fear which the film aroused, never justified, was that it would incite imitations. Brando played the nihilistic leader of the pack who vandalises the town but comes ultimately to owe something to the integrity of the citizenry. Basically it was moral tale, but in 1953 retribution had to be spelled out in capital letters. Johnny does not marry the girl (Mary Murphy), nor does he ride off into the sunset a converted soul. This alone was enough to panic the reactionary element and the ensuing controversy left no room for appreciation of the film's lean structure, the tight direction or the quality of the acting that could build such a slight storyline into a national incident. Johnny was indeed an archetypal Brando non-communicator and the equation of sexuality and violence (so commonly to be debased in future

This page: in Hang 'Em High.   Opposite: in the Eiger Sanction

years) was adroitly drawn. By the time the film was publicly released in Britain it was undeniably dated, but the power of the characterisation holds true.

On The Waterfront (his third collaboration with Kazan) marked the end of the first chapter in Brando's screen career. It is a justly famous film, applying the one-man-against-the-system heroics to the case of a docker's dawning awareness of the graft and corruption that surrounds him and his determination to smash the crooked union. But that is to simplify unfairly a first-rate script. Brando's study of guilt, of remorse, of failure, touched a chord in everyone and (supported brilliantly by Rod Steiger, Karl Malden and Eva Marie Saint) he gave the American cinema one of its truly great performances, one that does not date nor diminish with repeated viewings. One felt that the 1954 Oscar had been richly deserved and while that award (rejected by Brando when offered it a second time for *The Godfather*) crowned an era for the actor, the film marked his last meeting with public approval for quite a while.

His film career was in full swing – so was his private life. He has inspired violent contradictions in his love life: some ladies recall him fondly, others dismiss him derisively. His most lasting liaison – on the elastic terms on which he insists – is with Tahitian beauty Tarita whom he met while making *Mutiny on the Bounty* and by whom he has a son and daughter. He almost married a French model, Josanne Berenger, whom he had met in New York. One evening he told her to make supper for three and arrived with another girl. "Marlon enjoys humiliating women," says an acquaintance. While Marlon was making *Desirée*, Josanne was a constant visitor to the set but it was not a flamboyant romance, which was why there was an amazed reaction when Brando went to France and Josanne's parents announced their engagement. As well as amazement, there was the general feeling that the romance was just another of Marlon's brief encounters. Josanne gave interviews about Brando, went on television and won small roles in plays and films. But when Marlon lost interest, she slipped quietly away again.

After Josanne, Marlon went through a phase where he preferred actresses to unknowns. Shelley Winters, Pier Angeli, Joan Collins, Rita Moreno, France Nuyen were among his dates. A fiery romance with Movita (real name Maria Louisa Castenada), an actress who appeared in the first *Mutiny on the Bounty*, began during the filming of *Viva Zapata!* and

Opposite: the Oscar-winning appearance in The Godfather

continued off and on for many years. About the time he made *Sayonara* in Japan, Marlon was beginning to admit that he wanted to get married and have children, but everyone was surprised when he married Anna Kashfi on October 11, 1957 at the home of his aunt, Betty Lindemeyer, with whom he had lived when he first came to California.

Anna Kashfi always claimed she was Indian (knowing Marlon's penchant for the exotic and pandering to it) but, a day after the marriage, an Irishman said she was his daughter. It was not a happy marriage. Until the birth of their son, Christian Devi, on May 11, 1958, their private battles were kept out of the newspapers, but they separated soon after Christian's birth. Many years later Marlon went to the courts to fight for, and eventually gain, custody of his son. The curious quixotic nature of the man — half exhibitionist — half recluse, with his deep distrust of journalists and publicity, makes his public fights for his son all the more remarkable.

Anna Kashfi announced she was divorcing Marlon ten days prior to their first wedding anniversary. ("I can no longer take his indifference and his strange way of living.") During 1960 Marlon married Movita and they had a son, Miko. His relationships with other women continued, but the most lasting of these was with Tarita. Although Brando found plenty of time for women, they seem not to contribute greatly to his happiness — in fact one disenchanted girlfriend said his treatment of women would have fascinated Freud. His career is probably more important to him, almost certainly his causes are. He has always worked strenuously for the underdog: the Civil Rights Movement was helped by his support and he has championed the American Indian for some years.

At the box-office Brando became poisonous during the late '50s and early '60s. Film after film failed to excite the public while some critics remained faithful and believed he could still produce the goods if given the right material. The first film in the long decline had been *Desirée*, made simply because Brando (having fought shy of the title role in *The Egyptian*) now owed 20th Century-Fox a promised slice of historical hokum. It was a preposterous romance with Jean Simmons as the power behind the Napoleonic throne and Brando hamming handsomely as Bonaparte. It was made as a women's weepie and indeed the women wept. No more can be said. There followed two inspired pieces of casting, both

brought about at Brando's instigation. By rights they should have freed him forever from the label that Hollywood had given him. *Guys and Dolls* was a lengthy musical adaptation of the smash Broadway hit, based on the sharp Damon Runyon stories.

Brando was Sky Masterson, a king gambler who, for a bet, woos and finally wins a lady Salvationist (Jean Simmons again, the only leading actress ever to work twice with Brando). Some new songs were added and although neither Simmons nor Brando had any musical training, director Joseph L Mankiewicz remembered from his experience on *Julius Caesar* that Brando was a magician. Indeed he conjured up a slight baritone but made the songs score dramatically. Sadly, conflicting contracts with recording companies meant that there was no soundtrack album, but Brando is to be heard singing "Luck Be a Lady" and "A Woman in Love" (with Simmons) on an EP record. Nevertheless, despite its Broadway pedigree and the Brando-Simmons-Sinatra chemistry, *Guys and Dolls* was nowhere near the size of success that MGM had anticipated.

Neither was *The Teahouse of the August Moon*, though this stage play was altogether a more risky proposition. Brando was virtually unrecognisable under Oriental make-up as he played a wily, philosophical interpreter assigned to Glenn Ford's likeably ineffectual soldier. The escapades of the sympathetic couple gave Brando the freest rein yet for broad comedy and his last chance to smile on the screen until *Bedtime Story*. *Teahouse* was to have been made in Japan, but Hollywood stood in when torrential rains made location shooting impractical. Brando took the lead in *Sayonara* as his next assignment to assuage his disappointment. This ramshackle love story about American soldiers falling in love with and marrying Japanese girls, then being forbidden to bring their wives home to the States, was sluggishly directed by Joshua Logan. Red Buttons and Myoshi Umeki won Oscars as a doomed mixed-marriage couple. Brando and Miiko Taka survived the perils of their relationship and Brando's performance just survived the longueurs of the movie. Although it had some success in America, the film failed to capture the public imagination in Britain.

The Young Lions was, however, a considerable success for Brando. In Edward Dmytryk's multi-layered war epic (freely adapted from the Irwin Shaw novel) he played a young German officer gradually horrified by the senselessness

of the war he is all geared up to fight. The film followed his
career and that of a Jewish GI (Montgomery Clift), bringing
them together only in the final moment. So in effect Brando
was in a film by himself (with only Maximilian Schell as his
aide) and he gave a provocative and controversial reading of
the young Nazi — more sympathetic than the character was
in the book, and much more fully-rounded. But it was to be
his last international commercial success for nearly fifteen
years.

Insomuch as an actor is thought of as a box-office
commodity, these were the waning years. They got off to a
financially alarming start with the western *One Eyed Jacks*,
which Brando elected to direct. It was a relatively
straightforward revenge story that came to be overloaded
with significances that were never originally intended.
Brando's performance was hypnotic and, on face value, he
seemed a valuable recruit to direction. Sadly the matter could
not be left there: the film had run three times over schedule
and three times over budget because of Brando's insistent
perfectionism. It never recouped its estimated six million
dollar cost.

Back to "type" and back to Tennessee Williams in *The*

Above: with Maria Schneider in Last Tango in Paris

Fugitive Kind, Sidney Lumet's beautifully organised film of the play "Orpheus Descending". Brando was brash and enigmatic as the musician who breezes into town to keep a date with destiny as the fourth aspect of a triangle previously comprised of Anna Magnani's wretched, joy-starved storekeeper, Victor Jory's cancer-ridden tyrant and Joanne Woodward's blousy nymphomaniac. The story is too pretentious and overheated to rate with Williams' best work, but the performances went more than half way towards redeeming it.

The re-make of *Mutiny on the Bounty* with Brando in Clark Gable's original Fletcher Christian role (Trevor Howard was Captain Bligh) is probably the best documented film disaster of the '60s. Everything conspired to make it one of the most costly and unhappy flops of this period. *Mutiny on the Bounty* was almost as crisis-laden as Elizabeth Taylor's *Cleopatra*. Brando insisted on a change of director and, as he had artistic control, the studio were forced to listen while he changed his mind on any number of points. The budget for the film shot up to nineteen million dollars. The story goes that, during the making of *Mutiny on the Bounty*, he would wear ear plugs because the other actors distracted him. Trevor Howard would sooner not discuss him. Richard Harris has a deep dislike of him. When the final cut did come in, one year and many many millions of dollars later, the film was not half bad. Brando played Christian with a foppishness that many commentators construed as a gesture of contempt for the film. In fact it is easy to justify in the context of the character and it was extremely well sustained throughout the marathon running time.

Brando hadn't really flexed his political muscles in the movies for a decade when he elected to undertake *The Ugly American*. It was about American foreign policy and was set in a mythical Asian country to which Brando is sent as US Ambassador. It was extremely well written, and lent stature by the integrity of the performances, but producer-director George Englund did not sugar the pill sufficiently for audiences to swallow it. Brando was absolutely first class and the film rates as his most noble and worthwhile failure.

After the strains of *Mutiny on the Bounty* and the total commitment of *The Ugly American*, it is not difficult to see why a frothy confection like *Bedtime Story* appealed to Brando. He and David Niven played confidence tricksters out to part Shirley Jones from the fortune they imagined she

Opposite: in The Wild One

had. What was meant to be debonair came across as downright dull but this was basically the fault of lacklustre material. Many thought that Brando's main seduction ruse — feigning paralysis — was the height of bad taste. One could see their point.

Neither did audiences rally to the call of a rather heavy-handed spy thriller *The Saboteur: Code Name Morituri*. Brando was the spy aboard Captain Yul Brynner's German freighter taking a vital cargo to occupied France. *The Chase* fared better, though it was probably the reputation of director Arthur Penn rather than Brando's waning star appeal that brought the art-house audiences in to see the film. Brando was the sheriff of another absurdly overheated town in the Deep South. Tensions run high when a local boy breaks out of a nearby jail and is thought to have committed a murder in the course of the escape. Brando tries to stop mob rule and gets painfully beaten for his troubles. After the punishment he had handed himself in *One Eyed Jacks* (and the coming violence of *South-West to Sonora* and *Reflections in a Golden Eye*) some commentators wondered whether Brando now had a scene of personal violence written into his contract. Indeed the violence of *The Chase* was excessive though the film, and Brando, wielded a crude, cruel power.

In *South-West to Sonora*, Brando's gentle buffalo hunter is turned into a man of violence by revenge. Bandit John Saxon steals Brando's prize horse and has him viciously beaten. The actor's great physical presence was the only thing that distinguished an otherwise mundane western.

It did look as though Brando's streak of bad luck would be terminated by *A Countess From Hong Kong*, a film written and directed by Brando's idol, Charles Chaplin. It was also an out-and-out farce and Brando had proved in the past that he was rarely so good as when trying a new genre for the first time. But the sad truth is that the film was only mildly amusing and although Brando and Sophia Loren worked well together, not even their immaculate timing could justify one joke (a stowaway aristocrat) being stretched over nearly two hours. Audiences rejected its old-fashioned style.

When Marlon worked with Elizabeth Taylor on *Reflections in a Golden Eye* everyone predicted another of his personality clashes since it was the first time in many years that he had worked with a lady whose star stature was equal — if not greater — to his own. But the predicted fireworks did not occur. *Reflections in a Golden Eye* has enjoyed an

Opposite: in Michael Winner's The Nightcomers

underground cult success since its original release for, at the time, it was severely undervalued. Brando plays a miserable professional soldier, a latent homosexual saddled with a vulgarian wife (Elizabeth Taylor). Each is attracted by a young private (Robert Forster) and Brando misconstrues the boy's attention: he is obsessed with Miss Taylor. There is a tragic conclusion but, along the route, Brando fleshed out enormously well the tortured complexity of the character. Future generations will hopefully judge the film, and the performances, more kindly.

A regrettable appearance as a randy guru in the puerile *Candy* prefaced *The Night of the Following Day*, a kidnap thriller with Pamela Franklin as the hapless victim, Richard Boone as the sadistic criminal and Brando hovering equivocally between them. With the blondness of his hair accentuated and his wardrobe totally black, Brando stood out from the rest of the gang and the enigma of the character was never fully resolved. It was one of the more animal of his later performances, but again seen by too few people.

Queimada (or *Burn!*) was an attempt by Italian director Gillo Pontecorvo to take the political content of his prizewinning film *The Battle of Algiers* and place it into an acceptable narrative structure. Perhaps it was Brando's irresistible urge to support minority causes that brought him to this violent charade about an Englishman sent to a Portuguese colony to ferment a revolution. It was a signal failure and neither Brando nor Pontecorvo made a secret of their mutual animosity by the end of shooting.

Next came *The Nightcomers* in which Brando played the evil, sadistic valet, Quint. The screenplay was a prologue to Henry James' famous "The Turn of the Screw" and it suggested how Quint and the governess, Miss Jessel, became the spirits who possessed the children. It is an excellent performance of a man, as disturbed as he is disturbing. It also won Brando good notices across the board, his first enthusiastic set in quite a long time.

Fortunately for those who believe Brando to be the consummate screen actor, the theory that he was over the creative hill was disproved in the '70s. "People were always ready to say 'He's had it,' " comments Elia Kazan. "It makes me furious. Talent is delicate. It can hide for a while, go underground, get discouraged. It's human, but it never goes away."

It would have been the supreme irony if all Brando's

Opposite: in The Missouri Breaks

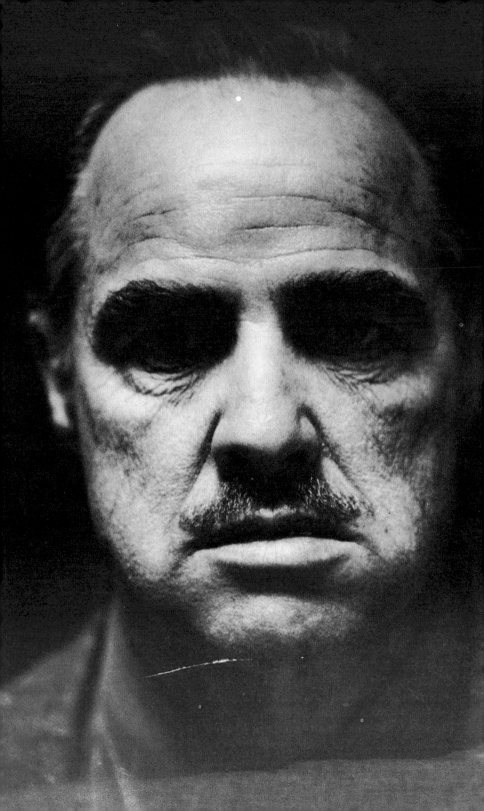

worthwhile box-office disappointments had barred him from his richly deserved stab at Don Corleone in *The Godfather*. There was talk of studio timidity, of other actors under consideration, but Brando was adamant. He auditioned with wads of cotton wool stuffed in his cheeks, the mumble for once a positive advantage. That he won the part is history. But the advanced reports of violence and bloodshed in this story of Mafia family life had not prepared one for the complexity and quality of a sprawling, massive masterpiece. Brando's performance was unique, even in his career of distinguished performances. *The Godfather* — made with a stringently enforced publicity embargo — re-established him as a superstar. He was nominated for Best Actor Oscar but created another typical Brando furore by having an Indian girl read a prepared statement refusing the Oscar when he did win.

Last Tango in Paris excited almost as much controversy, and confirmed Brando's commercial viability. The gifted young Italian director Bernardo Bertolucci, cast Brando and the unknown Maria Schneider as the animal lovers who indulge in an anonymous, purely physical affair in a barren Paris apartment.

On the considerable laurels of *The Godfather* and *Last Tango in Paris*, Brando could comfortably afford (quite literally) to rest. Again the hottest of box-office properties, producers queued up to offer him films, many canny enough to bait the offers with stories that championed minority causes. But Brando saw through them all and kept out of the limelight until Arthur Penn coaxed him to star in the western *The Missouri Breaks* with Jack Nicholson.

Brando had long been Nicholson's personal idol but, when the younger actor arrived on the set, he found that Brando had already pirated the film. The role of the relentless bounty hunter had been altered and enlarged: Nicholson's had been diminished. The film could have been saved in the cutting, but it wasn't. Though elegiac of tone, beautifully photographed and well played, it remains an oddball, unbalanced movie.

At the time of writing, two major projects are waiting to be seen and judged by the public — Francis Ford Coppola's *Apocalypse Now* and the long-planned *Superman* — and it seems probable that Brando will once more turn the tables on his critics and, through the late '70s, defend his title as one of Hollywood's most creative and original actors.

Opposite: as Don Corleone in The Godfather

worthwhile box-office disappointments had barred him from his richly deserved stab at Don Corleone in *The Godfather*. There was talk of studio timidity, of other actors under consideration, but Brando was adamant. He auditioned with wads of cotton wool stuffed in his cheeks, the mumble for once a positive advantage. That he won the part is history. But the advanced reports of violence and bloodshed in this story of Mafia family life had not prepared one for the complexity and quality of a sprawling, massive masterpiece. Brando's performance was unique, even in his career of distinguished performances. *The Godfather* — made with a stringently enforced publicity embargo — re-established him as a superstar. He was nominated for Best Actor Oscar but created another typical Brando furore by having an Indian girl read a prepared statement refusing the Oscar when he did win.

Last Tango in Paris excited almost as much controversy, and confirmed Brando's commercial viability. The gifted young Italian director Bernardo Bertolucci, cast Brando and the unknown Maria Schneider as the animal lovers who indulge in an anonymous, purely physical affair in a barren Paris apartment.

On the considerable laurels of *The Godfather* and *Last Tango in Paris*, Brando could comfortably afford (quite literally) to rest. Again the hottest box-office properties, producers queued up to offer him films, many canny enough to bait the offers with stories that championed minority causes. But Brando saw through them all and kept out of the limelight until Arthur Penn coaxed him to star in the western *The Missouri Breaks* with Jack Nicholson.

Brando had long been Nicholson's personal idol but, when the young actor arrived on the set, he found that Brando had already pirated the film. The role of the relentless bounty hunter had been altered and enlarged: Nicholson's had been diminished. The film could have been saved in the cutting, but it wasn't. Though elegiac of tone, beautifully photographed and well played, it remained an oddball, unbalanced movie. Amid huge controversy over the size of his fee (he received $3 million and later sued the producers over his gross percentage), Brando next appeared in *Superman*. He played Jor-El, the Kryptonian scientist who sent his son away to Earth to become Clark Kent, alias Superman. The film's budget spiralled up to $65 million but, for this unprecedented sum, producers Ilya Salkind and Pierre Spengler also gained

the basic material for the sequel, *Superman II* (in which, fo.
legal and contractual reasons Brando does *not* appear, evei
though that film opens with a lengthy flashback). Anothe
expensive production followed, Francis Coppola'
Apocalypse Now, in which Brando once more played a smal
but key part — that of Colonel Kurtz, the crazed an
genocide-waging soldier whose command Martin Sheen i
sent to terminate. After these two major productions,
Brando's next appearance was as a venal oil magnat
dedicated to the suppression of a formula for synthetic fuel i
The Formula. This was a lightweight and unremarkabl
thriller, but the preceding films had once again proved tha
this most mercurial and unpredictable of actors could still tur
the tables on his critics and, even into the '80s, defend hi
reputation as one of Hollywood's most creative and origina
talents.

PORTRAIT GALLERY

On the following pages we are presenting a gallery of portraits of Marlon Brando in the following order:

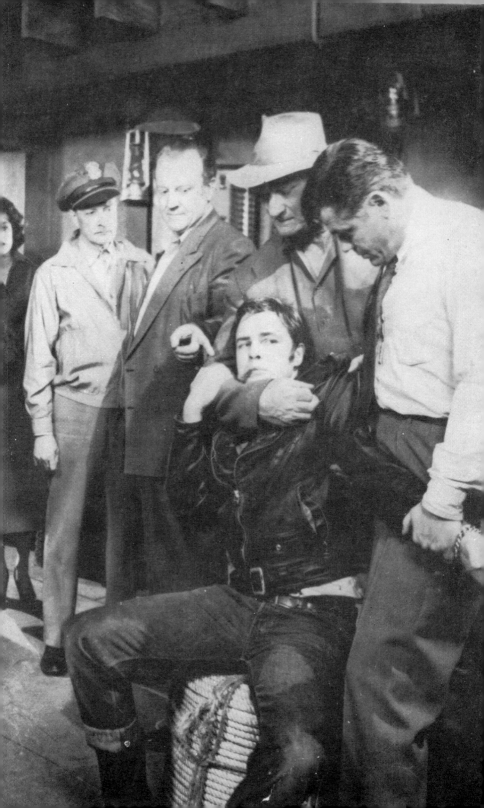

This page: in "A Streetcar Named Desire"

THE MEN (US 1950)

Prod/Stanley Kramer. Dir/Fred Zinneman. Scr/Carl
Foreman. Music/Dimitri Tiomkin. Ph/Robert de Grasse.
B&W. GB distribution/United Artists. Certificate A.
87 mins.
With: Marlon Brando (Ken), Teresa Wright (Ellen), Everett
Sloane (Dr Brock), Jack Webb (Norm), Richard Erdman
(Leo)
The Men marked Brando's début film appearance, after
which he was hailed by studio publicists as "the actor who
would make Holywood revise its standards of performances."
This vivid semi-documentary has Brando as an ex-GI trying to
come to terms with disability after being shot in the back
during the war and left paralysed from the waist down. The
film follows his initial reaction of disbelief,
self-pity and withdrawal, to a growing determination to lead
as normal a life as possible. Having broken off his
engagement, he decides to go through with the marriage to his
girlfriend (Teresa Wright) and, in so doing, realises that his
wife has her own problems in learning to cope with a
paraplegic husband.

STREETCAR NAMED DESIRE (US 1951)

Prod/Charles K Feldman. Dir/Elia Kazan. Scr/Tennessee
Williams based on his play, adapted by Oscar Saul. Music/
Alex North. Ph/Harry Stradling. B&W. GB distribution/
Columbia-Warner (Warner). Certificate X. 121 mins.
With: Vivien Leigh (Blanche), Marlon Brando (Stanley),
Kim Hunter (Stella), Karl Malden (Mitch), Rudy Bond
(Steve), Nick Dennis (Pablo), Peg Hillias (Eunice), Wright
King (A collector), Richard Garrick (Doctor), Anne Dere
(Matron)
Having set the New York stage alight with his portrayal of
Stanley Kowalski in "A Streetcar Named Desire," Brando
repeated his role when Elia Kazan came to translate his stage
production on to film. Based on Tennessee Williams's prizewinning play, it's the story of Blanche Dubois (Viven Leigh),
a destitute and gently demented Southern belle who brings
her daydreams of faded gentility to the drab home of her
younger sister Stella (Kim Hunter), and her brutish husband
Stanley. Mean and vindictive, Stanley has little time for his
sister-in-law who, during her stay with them, adds to the trail
of destruction she has left behind all her life.

VIVA ZAPATA! (US 1952)
Prod/Darryl F Zanuck. Dir/Elia Kazan. Scr/John Steinbeck.
Music/Alex North. Ph/Joe Macdonald. B&W. GB distribution/
20th Century-Fox. Certificate A. 113 mins.
With: Marlon Brando (Zapata), Jean Peters (Josefa),
Anthony Quinn (Eufemio), Joseph Wiseman (Fernando),
Arnold Moss (Don Nacio), Alan Reed (Pancho Villa), Margo
(Soldadera), Harold Gordon (Madera), Lou Gilbert (Pablo),
Frank Silvera (Huerta)
This vibrant film again directed by Elia Kazan, stars Brando
as Mexican revolutionary Emiliano Zapata, an outlaw who,
urged on by his ambitious wife Josefa (Jean Peters) and
backed by a small band of men, rises to power and eventual
Presidency. Anthony Quinn gives an Oscar-winning
performance as his brother Eufemio, who leads Zapata into
trouble with his obsession for power, finally causing him once
again to become a fugitive — destined for a violent end.

JULIUS CAESAR (US 1953)
Prod/John Houseman. Dir/Joseph L Mankiewicz. Scr/the
play by William Shakespeare. Music/Miklos Rozsa. Ph/Joseph
Ruttenberg. B&W. GB distribution/CIC (MGM). Certificate
U. 121 mins.

With: Marlon Brando (Mark Antony), James Mason (Brutus), John Gielgud (Cassius), Louis Calhern (Julius Caesar), Edmond O'Brien (Casca), Greer Garson (Calpurnia), Deborah Kerr (Portia), George Macready (Marcellus), Michael Pate (Flavius), Alan Napier (Cicero)

Despite misgivings about the casting of Brando as Mark Antony in *Julius Caesar*, the young actor delighted critics and the public by proving that he could both articulate the English poetry and hold his own alongside other more established players. In this superior adaptation of Shakespeare's play about political intrigue and personal honour in ancient Rome, James Mason, John Gielgud and Edmund O'Brien lead the conspirators who assassinate Caesar.

THE WILD ONE (US 1953)

Prod/Stanley Kramer. Dir/Laslo Benedek. Scr/John Paxton, based on a story by Frank Rooney. Music/Leith Stevens. Ph/ Hal Mohr. B&W. GB distribution/Columbia-Warner (Columbia). Certificate X. 79 mins.

With: Marlon Brando (Johnny), Mary Murphy (Kathie), Robert Keith (Harry Bleeker), Lee Marvin (Chino), Jay C Flippen (Sheriff Singer), Peggy Maley (Mildred), Hugh Sanders (Charlie Thomas), Ray Teal (Frank Bleeker), Will Wright (Art Kleiner), Yvonne Doughty (Britches), Gene Peterson (Crazy), Alvy Moore (Pigeon)

Based on a true incident, *The Wild One* was the forerunner of today's bike movies. Brando plays Johnny, inarticulate leader of the Black Rebels Motorcycle club, who leads his gang into a small town where they terrorise the citizens during the course of a weekend. Local cop Harry (Robert Keith) fails to control the riders, especially when they are confronted by a rival gang led by Chino (Lee Marvin). The county sheriff eventually restores order in the town, but not before a man is accidentally killed by Johnny. A *cause célèbre* throughout America, the film also remained banned in Britain until 1968, becuase the hoodlum character of Johnny received no retribution for his actions.

ON THE WATERFRONT (US 1954)

Prod/Sam Spiegel. Dir/Elia Kazan. Scr/Buddy Schulberg, suggested by articles by Malcolm Johnson. Ph/Leonard Bernstein. Ph/Boris Kaufman. B&W. GB distribution/ Columbia-Warner (Columbia). Certificate A. 107 mins.

With: Marlon Brando (Terry Malloy), Eva Marie Saint (Edie

Doyle), Karl Marlden (Father Barry), Lee J Cobb (Johnny Friendly), Rod Steiger (Charley Malloy), Pat Henning (Kayo Dugan), Leif Erickson (Glover), James Westerfield (Big Mac), John Heldebrand (Mutt), Rudy Bond (Moose), John Hamilton (Pop Doyle)

That Brando was an actor of rare power and sensitivity was confirmed by *On the Waterfront*, for which he won the first of his two Oscars. He plays Terry Malloy, a none-too-bright, slightly punch-drunk ex-boxer who lives on the edge of dockyard corruption in New York, and indirectly benefits from it through his brother Charlie (Rod Steiger), one of the henchmen of underworld union boss Johnny Friendly (Lee J Cobb). With this powerful and much-imitated film, the relationship between Elia Kazan and Brando reached its productive zenith, and many consider the actor's performance to be the finest of his career.

DESIRÉE (US 1954)

Prod/Julien Blaustein. Dir/Henry Koster. Scr/Daniel Taradash, based on the novel by Annemarie Selinko. Music/ Alex North. Ph/Milton Krasner. Colour by DeLuxe. GB distribution/20th Century-Fox. Certificate A. 110 mins.

With: Marlon Brando (Napoleon), Jean Simmons (Desirée), Merle Oberon (Josephine), Michael Rennie (Bernadotte), Cameron Mitchell (Joseph Bonaparte), Elizabeth Sellers (Julie), Charlotte Austin (Paulette), Cathleen Nesbitt (Mademoiselle Bonaparte)

Desirée, with Jean Simmons in the title role, is a muddled and fictionalised account of the rise and fall of French Emperor Napoleon Bonaparte (Brando) whose first love, Desirée, was a driving force behind his ambitious career. The film performed disappointingly at the box-office, Brando having made it simply because he owed 20th Century-Fox a costume drama, after walking out on their project *The Egyptian*. That film was eventually made with Edmund Purdom taking the Brando role.

GUYS AND DOLLS (US 1955)

Prod/Samuel Goldwyn. Dir-scr/Joseph L Mankiewicz, based on the play by Joe Swerling and Abe Burrows. Music/Frank Loesser. Ph / Harry Stradling. Eastman Colour. GB distribution/CIC (MGM). Certificate A. 149 mins.

With: Marlon Brando (Sky Masterson), Jean Simmons (Sarah Brown), Frank Sinatra (Nathan Detroit), Vivian

Blaine (Adelaid), Stubby Kaye (Nicely Nicely Johnson), Johnny Silver (Benny Southstreet), B S Pully (Big Jule), Sheldon Leonard (Harry the Horse), Robert Keith (Lt Brannigan)

Both Frank Sinatra and Marlon Brando were criticised as being miscast in this lavish musical comedy about a gambler called Sky Masterson (Brando), who takes on a £1,000 bet to woo a lady Salvationist (Jean Simmons). Hoping that he'll lose the bet is Nathan Detroit (Sinatra), another gambler who needs the money to keep his floating crap game in existence. Although Brando had never had any formal musical training, he managed to conjure up an adequate baritone, and gave a fairly enjoyable rendition of "Luck Be a Lady." The film, however, was nowhere near the success that MGM had hoped.

TEAHOUSE OF THE AUGUST MOON (US 1956)
Prod/Jack Cummings. Dir/Daniel Mann. Scr/John Patrick, based on the book by Vera Sneider and the play by John Patrick. Music/Saul Chaplin. Ph/John Alton. Metrocolor. GB distribution/CIC (MGM). Certificate U. 123 mins.
With: Marlon Brando (Sakani), Glenn Ford (Captain Fisby), Machito Kyo (Lotus Blossom), Eddie Albert (Captain McLean), Paul Ford (Colonel Pindy), Jun Negami (Mr Seiko), Nijiko Kujokawa (Miss Higa Jiga)
Virtually unrecognisable under heavy Oriental make-up, Brando plays Sakini, a wily Okinawan interpreter who helps Army officers Fisby (Glenn Ford) and McLean (Eddie Albert) succumb to the local way of life in American-occupied Japan. The movie was to have been made on location, but Hollywood stood in when torrential seasonal rains made shooting impossible.

SAYONARA (US 1957)
Prod/William Goetz. Dir/Joshua Logan. Scr/Paul Osborn, based on the novel by James A Michener. Music/Franz Waxman. Song/Irving Berlin. Ph/Ellsworth Fredericks. Technicolor. GB distribution/Columbia-Warner (Warner). Certificate A. 147 mins.
With: Marlon Brando (Major Lloyd Gruver), Miiko Tak (Hana-ogi), Red Buttons (Airman Joe Kelly), Patricia Owens (Eileen Webster), Ricardo Montalban (Nakamura), Myoshi Umeki (Katsumi), Kent Smith (General Webster), Martha Scott (Mrs Webster), James Garner (Captain

This page: in "Mutiny on the Bounty"

Bailey), Doug Watson (Colonel Calhoun)

Sayonara made up for Brando's earlier disappointment at not getting to Japan by being shot entirely on location there. A great success at the time, especially with American audiences, it had Brando and Red Buttons as two US soldiers who fall in love with and marry Japanese girls, then encounter racial prejudice when they contemplate returning home to America with their wives. The film won four of the nine Academy Awards for which it was nominated, including those for cinematography and art direction. Although Brando didn't win his category, Red Buttons and Miyoshi Umeki deservedly carried off a statue each for their memorable supporting roles.

THE YOUNG LIONS (US 1958)

Prod/Al Lichtman. Dir/Edward Dmytryk. Scr/Edward Anhalt, based on the novel by Irwin Shaw. Music/Hugo Friedhofer. Ph/Joe MacDonald. B&W. GB distribution/20th Century-Fox. Certificate A. 167 mins.

With: Marlon Brando (Christian Diestl), Montgomery Clift (Noah Ackerman), Dean Martin (Michael Whiteacre), Hope Lange (Hope Plowman), Barbara Rush (Margaret Freemantle), May Britt (Gretchen Hardenberg), Maxmilian Schell (Hardenberg), Dora Doll (Simone), Lee Van Cleef (Sgt Rickett), Arthur Franz (Lt Green)

The three-way plot of this multi-layered war epic concerns an entertainer (Dean Martin) drafted into the Army but trying to dodge active combat; a Jewish GI (Montgomery Clift) who encounters racial prejudice among his fellow servicemen; and a confused Nazi (Brando) who joins Hitler's army to get ahead in a stratified society, only to be revolted by the misery and suffering caused by his ruthless ambitions. Although Clift and Brando shared no scenes together, the film drew its strength from the competition between them, as they vied for centre stage. Brando had wanted the film to end with a shot of himself spreadeagled on a makeshift cross of barbed-wire, to symbolise the dramatic change of heart he undergoes, but Clift objected and managed to overrule him. At the time one observer remarked: "No one gets to play Jesus in a movie if Clift is in it."

ONE EYED JACKS (US 1960)

Prod/Frank P Rosenberg. Dir/Marlon Brando. Scr/Guy Trosper, Calder Willingham, based on the novel "The

Authentic Death of Hendry Jones" by Charles Neider. Music/
Hugo Friedhofer. Ph/Charles Lang Jnr. Technicolor. GB
distribution/CIC (Paramount). Certificate A. 141 mins.
With: Marlon Brando (Rio), Karl Malden (Dad Longworth),
Pina Pellicer (Louisa), Katy Jurado (Maria), Ben Johnson
(Bob Amory), Slim Pickens (Lon), Larry Duran (Modesto),
Sam Gilman (Harvey), Timothy Carey (Howard Tetley)
In Sonora, circa 1885, Rio the Kid (Brando) and Dad
Longworth (Karl Malden) are outlaws on the run after
robbing a bank. Dad betrays Rio, who spends five years in jail
before managing to escape. Seething with revenge he tracks
downs Dad, now a respectable sheriff with a wife (Katy
Jurado) and step-daughter Luisa (Pina Pellicer). As part of
his revenge, he deliberately seduces Luisa, but receives a
public thrashing when the sheriff finds out. Threatening to
come back and kill Dad, he is torn between avenging the past
and his new-found love for Luisa.

THE FUGITIVE KIND (US 1960)
Prod/Martin Jurow, Richard A Shepard. Scr/Sidney Lumet.
Scr/Tennessee Williams, Meade Roberts, based on Williams'
play "Orpheus Descending." Music/Kenyon Hopkins. Ph/
Boris Kaufman. GB distribution/United Artists. Certificate
X. 121 mins.
With: Marlon Brando (Val Xavier), Anna Magnani (Lady
Torrance), Joanne Woodward (Carol Cutrere), Maureen
Stapleton (Vee Talbot), Victor Jory (Jabe Torrance), R G
Armstrong (Sherrif Talbot), Emory Richardson (Uncle
Pleasant), Spivy (Ruby Lightfoot)
When *The Fugitive Kid* was in pre-production stage, Brando
became the first actor ever to be offered a salary of one
million dollars. His part was that of Val Xavier, a drifter who
arrives in a small town and gets a job in a store run by Lady
Torrence (Anna Magnani), a sexually repressed woman
whose husband is dying of cancer. Val is attracted to her
maturity and grace, but at the same time is pursued by Carol
(Joanne Woodward), the enigmatic but spunky local tramp
who tries to seduce him.

MUTINY ON THE BOUNTY (US 1962)
Prod/Aaron Rosenberg. Dir/Lewis Milestone. Scr/Charles
Lederer, based on the novel by Charles Nordhoff and James
Norman Hall. Music/Bronislau Kaper. Ph/Robert L Surtees.
Technicolor. GB distribution/CIC (MGM). Certificate A.

178 mins (from 185).

With: Marlon Brando (Fletcher Christian) Trevor Howard (William Bligh), Richard Harris (John Mills), Hugh Griffith (Alexander Smith), Richard Haydn (William Brown), Tim Seely (Edward Young), Percy Herbert (Matthew Quintal), Gordon Jackson (Edward Birkett), Chips Rafferty (Michael Byrne), Eddie Byrne (John Fryer), Frank Silvera (Minarii), Ben Wright (Graves), Torin Thatcher (Staines), Tarita (Maimiti)

This budget-busting, crisis-laden remake of the successful 1935 version (starring Charles Laughton and Clark Gable), was one of the major film disasters of the '60s, preceding by a year, Elizabeth Taylor's colossal flop, *Cleopatra*. Brando refused to play Fletcher Christian as Gable had: a rough, practical man turned reluctant hero, and instead portrayed him as high-minded, aristocratic, intellectual and foppish. His battle with the crude, uneducated and despised Captain Bligh (Trevor Howard) was a bout between opposing classes. Brando has possibly the longest death scene in cinema history, and in the wake of the débâcle, MGM stock dropped ten points while the anti-Brando press had a field day with colourful stories about the distressed studio under siege by an unreasonable star.

THE UGLY AMERICAN (US 1962)

Prod-dir/George Englund. Scr/Stewart Stern, based on the novel by William J Lederer and Eugene Burdick. Music/Frank Skinner. Ph/Clifford Stine. Eastman Colour. GB distribution/ Rank. Certificate U. 120 mins.

With: Marlon Brando (Harrison Carter Macwhite), Eiji Okada (Deong), Sandra Church (Marion Macwhite), Pat Hingle (Homer Atkins), Arthur Hill (Grainer), Jocelyn Brando (Emma Atkins), Kikrit Pramoj (Prime Minister)

Uncannily prophetic about the American involvement in Vietnam, this heavily political film takes place in the mythical country of Sarkhan, somewhere in South-East Asia. Harrison MacWhite (Brando), who knows the country well through previous wartime activities there, arrives as the newly appointed US Ambassador. Minutes after his arrival he has a frightening encounter with an angry mob of anti-American demonstrators containing pro-Communist supporters. When Sarkhan erupts into flaming civil war, it is soon clear that the puppet régime, installed by the Americans, will not survive.

Opposite: in Superman — The Movie

BEDTIME STORY (US 1964)

Prod/Stanley Shapiro. Dir/Ralph Levy. Scr/Stanley Shapiro, Paul Henning. Music/Hans J Salter. Ph/Clifford Stine. Eastman Colour. GB distribution/Rank. Certificate A. 99 mins.

With: Marlon Brando (Fred Benson), David Niven (Lawrence Jamison), Shirley Jones (Janet Walker), Dody Goodman (Fanny Eubank), Aram Stephan (Monsieur Andre)

Brando plays Benson, a small-time confidence trickster who specialises in hit-and-run seduction by travelling through Germany posing as an American GI of Teutonic extraction. Benson is content until he reaches the Riviera where he meets Jamison (David Niven), a professional operator who not only gets women to share his bed but also to bestow their jewels on him for fake revolutionary causes. Keen to join the sex-plus-finance market, Benson forms a partnership with Jamison, whereupon they attempt to part American soap queen Janet Walker (Shirley Jones) from the fortune they imagine she possesses. The movie was widely criticised for scenes of bad taste, the London "Daily Express" calling it, "the most vulgar and embarrassing film of the year."

THE SABOTEUR — CODE NAME MORITURI (Original title: Morituri) (US 1965)

Prod/Aaron Rosenberg. Dir/Bernhard Wicki. Scr/Daniel Taradash, based on the novel by Werner Joerg Luedecke. Music/Jerry Goldsmith. Ph/Conrad Hall. B&W. GB distribution/20th Century-Fox. Certificate A. 122 mins.

With: Marlon Brando (Robert Crain), Yul Brynner (Captain Mueller), Janet Margolin (Esther), Trevor Howard (Colonel Statter), Martin Benrath (Kruse), Hans Christian Blech (Donkeyman), Wally Cos (Dr Ambach)

In 1942, a rich anti-Nazi German (Brando) is persuaded by a British agent (Trevor Howard) to board a blockade runner carrying a vital cargo en route from Japan to occupied France. Yul Brynner plays the captain of the freighter, who discovers that Brando is not the pacifist he claims to be, but an undercover spy on a mission of sabotage.

THE CHASE (US 1965)

Prod/Sam Spiegel. Scr/Arthur Penn. Scr/Lillian Hellman, based on the novel by Horton Foote. Music/John Barry. Ph/Joseph LaShelle. Technicolor. GB distribution/Columbia-

Opposite: with Susannah York in Superman — The Movie

Warner (Columbia). Certificate X. 122 mins.
With: Marlon Brando (Calder), Jane Fonda (Anna Reeves), Robert Redford (Bubber Reeves), E G Marshall (Val Rogers), Angie Dickinson (Ruby Calder), Janice Rule (Emily Stewart), Miriam Hopkins (Mrs Reeves), Martha Hyer (Mary Fuller), Richard Bradford (Damon Fuller), Robert Duvall (Edwin Stewart), James Fox (Jake Rogers), Diana Hyland (Elizabeth Rogers), Henry Hull (Briggs), Jocelyn Brando (Mrs Briggs)

In Arthur Penn's excessively violent film, Brando plays Calder, an honourable but simple man who is appointed sheriff of a small Southern town run by powerful tycoon Val Rogers (E G Marshall). Tensions run high when local rebel Bubber Reeves (Robert Redford) escapes from a nearby chain-gang. As he makes his way towards town, Calder is put under pressure by Rogers to capture him before he reaches his wife (Jane Fonda) and discovers that she has been having an affair with the tycoon's son (James Fox). With Lillian Hellman complaining that her original screenplay had been destroyed in the finished production, and Penn claiming that his film had been ruinously edited in London, *The Chase* was disowned by one and all and had an inglorious commerical career. As one critic remarked: "Considering all the talent connected with it, it is hard to imagine how *The Chase* went so haywire."

THE APPALOOSA (GB: SOUTHWEST TO SONORA) (US 1965)

Prod/Alan Miller. Dir/Sidney J Furie. Scr/James Bridges, Roland Kibbee, based on the novel "The Appaloosa" by Robert MacLeod. Music/Frank Skinner. Ph/Russell Metty. Technicolor. GB distribution/Rank. Certificate A. 98 mins.
With: Marlon Brando (Matt), Anjanette Comer (Trini), John Saxon (Chuy), Rafael Campos (Paco), Miriam Colon (Ana), Emilio Fernandez (Lazaro), Alex Montoya (Squint-Eye), Frank Silvera (Ramos), Larry D Mann (Priest)

This slow-paced western had Brando playing a dignified buffalo hunter who abandons his trade to start his own cattle ranch. When a Mexican bandit (John Saxon) steals his prize stallion and viciously horse-drags him, Brando is turned from a gentle rancher into a man of fury and violence, hell-bent on revenge.

This page: in Queimada

A COUNTESS FROM HONG KONG (GB 1966)

Prod/Jerome Epstein. Dir-scr-music/Charles Chaplin. Ph/ Arthur Ibbetson. Technicolor. GB distribution / Rank. Certificate A. 120 mins.

With: Marlon Brando (Ogden), Sophia Loren (Natascha), Sidney Chaplin (Harvey), Tippi Hedren (Martha), Patrick Cargill (Hudson), Michael Medwin (John Felix), Oliver Johnston (Clark), John Paul (The Captain), Angela Scoular (The Society Girl), Margaret Rutherford (Miss Gaulswallow), Charles Chaplin (An Old Steward)

After a long retirement in Switzerland, Brando's idol — Charles Chaplin — returned to the cameras to direct the star in this ill-fated, lacklustre comedy. Sophia Loren is the destitute exiled Russian Countess who managed to escape from the Hong Kong police on a charge of prostitution, by hiding aboard a ship that belongs to an American millionaire (Brando). When he discovers and falls in love with his stowaway, complications arise when his wife boards the ship during a stop-over in Hawaii.

REFLECTIONS IN A GOLDEN EYE (US 1967)

Prod/Ray Stark. Dir/John Huston. Scr/Chapman Mortimer,

Gladys Hill, based on the novel by Carson McCullers. Music/ Toshiro Mayuzumi. Ph/Aldo Tonti. Technicolor. GB distribution/Columbia-Warner (Warner). Certificate X. 109 mins.

With: Marlon Brando (Major Weldon Penderton), Elizabeth Taylor (Leonora Penderton), Brian Keith (Lt Col Morris Langdon), Julie Harris (Alison Langdon), Zorro David (Anacleto), Robert Forster (Private Williams)

This film version of Carson McCullers' novella had originally been planned for Montgomery Clift, but after the actor's death in 1966, Brando took the central role. The predicted clashes of personality between Elizabeth Taylor and himself did not flare up in this film about an Army Major who comes tortuously to realise that he is a latent homosexual. Tragedy arises when he misconstrues the attention of a young private (Robert Forster) who is in fact obsessed with the Major's wife Leonora (Elizabeth Taylor).

CANDY (US/Italy/France 1968)

Prod/Robert Haggiag. Dir/Christian Marquand. Scr/Buck Henry, based on the novel by Terry Southern, Mason Hoffenberg. Music/Dave Grusin. Ph/Giuseppe Rotunno. Technicolor. GB distribution/CIRO. Certificate X. 122 mins (from 124 mins).

With: Ewa Aulin (Candy), Marlon Brando (Grindl), Richard Burton (McPhisto), James Coburn (Dr Krankeit), Walter Matthau (General Smight), Charles Asnavour (The Hunchback), John Huston (Dr Dunlap), John Astin (Daddy/ Uncle Jack), Elsa Martinelli (Livia), Ringo Starr (Emmanuel), Enrico Maria Salerno (Jonathan J John), Sugar Ray Robinson (Zero), Anita Pallenberg (Nurse Bullock), Lea Padovani (Silvia), Florinda Bolkan (Lolita)

This was a curious and often surreal tale about a girl on a trail of innocent corruption. An international cast did a series of star turns, with Brando appearing in his segment as a randy guru who finally gets caught in an avalanche and is turned into a glistening stalagmite. "Hippy psychedelics are laid on with the self-destroying effect of an overdose of garlic" commented the Monthly Film Bulletin.

THE NIGHT OF THE FOLLOWING DAY (US 1968)

Prod/Hubert Cornfield. Dir/Hubert Cornfield, Robert Phippeny, based on the novel "The Snatchers" by Lionel White. Music/Stanley Myers. Ph/Willy Kurant. Technicolor.

Opposite: as Jor-El in Superman

GB distribution/Rank. Certificate X. 93 mins.
With: Marlon Brando (Bud), Richard Boone (Leer), Rita
Morena (Vi), Pamela Franklin (The Girl), Jess Hahn
(Wally), Gerard Buhr (The Gendarme), Hugues Wanner
(The Father), Jacques Marin (Bartender), Al Lettieri (Pilot)
A teenage heiress (Pamela Franklin) arrives in Paris and is
kidnapped by her father's chauffeur (Brando), who takes her
off to a remote beach house on the coast of Normandy.
Chauffeur (the only name by which Brando's character is
known), is in league with a sadistic killer called Leer, a
cocaine addict named Vi, and her moronic brother Wally.

QUEIMADA! (US: BURN!) (Italy/France 1968)
Prod/Alberto. Grimaldi. Dir/Gillo Pontecorvo. Scr/Franco
Solinas, Giorgio Arlorio, from a story by Gillo Pontecorvo,
Franco Solinas, Giorgio Arlorio. Music/Ennion Morricone.
Ph/Marcello Gatti, Giuseppe Bruzzolini. Technicolor. GB
distribution/United Artists. Certificate AA. 112 mins.
With: Marlon Brando (Sir William Walker), Evaristo
Marquez (Jose Dolores), Renato Salvatori (Teddy Sanchez),
Norman Hill (Shelton), Gianpiero Albertini (Henry), Carlo
Palmucci (Jack), Cecily Browne (Lady Bella), Dana Ghia
(Francesca), Mauricio Rodriguez (Ramon), Alejandro
Obregon (English Major)
Brando's irresistible urge to support minority causes brought
him to this violent account of how an English diplomat named
William Walker (Brando) is sent to an imaginary Portuguese
colony called Queimada as an *agent provocateur,* to break up
a sugar-trade monopoly and incite revolution. He is
successful, and the Spanish-owned Caribbean island wins its
independence. Ten years later, Walker is sent back to the
colony to suppress black rebels, and is disillusioned to find
that the British have since taken it over. With paranoid zeal,
he sets about destroying his own creation.

THE NIGHTCOMERS (GB 1971)
Prod-dir/Michael Winner. Scr/Michael Hastings, based on
characters created by Henry James. Music/Jerry Fielding. Ph/
Robert Paynter. Technicolor. GB distribution/Avco-
Embassy. Certificate X. 96 mins.
With: Marlon Brando (Peter Quint), Stephanie Beacham
(Miss Jessel), Thora Hird (Mrs Grose), Harry Andrews
(Master of the House), Verna Harvey (Flora), Christopher
Ellis (Miles), Anna Palk (New Governess)

*This page: as
Colonel Kirtz in
Apocalypse
Now*

A prologue to Henry James's famous "The Turn of the Screw," the film tells how that story's two young children, Flora and Miles, fall under the influence of Quint (Brando) and Miss Hessel (Stephanie Beacham), the gardener and governess whose spirits later come to possess them. The children, whose parents have both been killed in a car accident begin to ape the patterns of the couple's troubled sex life.

THE GODFATHER (US 1971)

Prod/Albert S Ruddy. Dir/Francis Ford Coppola. Scr/Mario Puzo, Francis Ford Coppola, based on Puzo's novel. Music/ Nino Rota. Ph/Gordon Willis. Technicolor. GB distribution/ CIC (Paramount). Certificate X. 175 mins.

With: Marlon Brando (Don Vito Corleone), Al Pacino (Michael Corleone), James Caan (Sonny Corleone), Richard Castellano (Clemenza), Robert Duvall (Tom Hagen), Sterling Hayden (McCluskey), John Marley (Jack Woltz), Richard Conte (Barzini), Diane Keaton (Kay Addams), Al Lettieri (Sollozzo), Abe Vigoda (Tessio), Talia Shire (Connie Rizzi), Gianni Russo (Carlo Rizzi), John Cazale (Fredo Corleone), Rudy Bond (Cuneo), Al Martino (Johnny Fontaine), Lenny Montana (Luca Brasi), Salvatore Corsitto (Bonasera), Alex Rocco (Moe Greene), Tony Giorgio (Bruno Tattaglia), Vito Scotti (Nazorine), Tere Livrano (Theresa Hagen), Victor Rendina (Phillip Tattaglia), Julie Gregg (Sandra Corleone), Jeannie Linero (Lucy Mancini), Ardell Sheridan (Mrs Clemenza)

One of the highest grossers in box-office history, Francis Coppola's sprawling masterpiece re-established Brando as one of the outstanding screen originals of the century. In the title role Brando gives a performance hailed as one of his greatest, as Don Corleone, the ageing Mafia Godfather who, after ruling New York's underworld for nearly two generations, has the problem of succession foremost in his realm. Equally brilliant is Al Pacino's supporting role as young Michael Corleone, the son intended to escape the family stranglehold of violence and vendettas, but who finds himself drawn ruthlessly into the vortex when gang warfare decimates his family. "Time" magazine described *The Godfather* as "a movie which seems to have everything … warmth, violence, nostalgia and the dynastic sweep of an Italian–American *Gone With The Wind.*" Brando was named as the winner of the Best Actor Oscar for 1971, but created

another typical furor by boycotting the awards ceremony
when he sent a militant Apache actress, Sasheen
Littlefeather, to decline the award.

L'ULTIMO TANGO A PARIGI (US/GB: LAST TANGO IN PARIS) (Italy/France 1972)

Prod/Alberto Grimaldi. Dir/Bernardo Bertolucci, Franco
Arcalli. Music/Gato Barbieri. Ph/Vittorio Storaro.
Technicolor. GB distribution/United Artists. Certificate X.
129 mins.
With: Marlon Brando (Paul), Maria Schneider (Jeanne),
Jean Pierre Leaud (Tom), Darling Legitimus (Concierge),
Catherine Sola (TV script girl), Mauro Marchetti (TV
cameraman), Dan Diament (TV sound engineer), Peter
Schommer (TV assistant cameraman), Catherine Allegret
(Catherine), Marie Helen Breillat (Monique), Catherine
Breillat (Mouchette)
From the moment Bernardo Bertolucci's compelling film first
erupted on to the screen, *Last Tango in Paris* has earned itself
a reputation as one of the most controversial movies of all
time. The story is a simple one. Paul (Brando) and Jeanne
(Maria Schneider) meet by chance in an empty Paris
apartment in which they suddenly and passionately make
love. Following the erotic encounter, the couple have
subsequent meetings at the apartment where they embark
upon an anonymous, purely physical affair, agreeing never to
talk about their lives or reveal their names. Outside, in
contemporary Paris, we follow them separately into their
private worlds where Jeanne is about to be married to a dull
young television film-maker, and Paul is seeking to
understand the recent unexplained suicide of his wife. The
film, which many say is without doubt Brando's most personal
and revealing, brought the actor the threat of prosecution
under Italian law for alleged indecencies committed on
screen.

THE MISSOURI BREAKS (US 1976)

Prod/Robert M Sherman. Dir/Arthur Penn. Scr/Thomas
McGuane. Music/John Williams. Ph/Michael Butler. Colour
by DeLuxe. GB distribution/United Artists. Certificate AA.
126 mins.
With: Marlon Brando (Robert Lee Clayton), Jack Nicholson
(Tom Logan), Randy Quaid (Little Tod), Kathleen Lloyd
(Jane Braxton), Frederic Forrest (Cary), Harry Dean

This page: with George C. Scott in The Formula

Stanton (Calvin), John McLiam (David Braxton), John Ryan
(Si), Sam Gilman (Hank Rate). Steve Franken (The
Lonesome Kid), Richard Bradford (Pete Marker), James
Greene (Hellsgate rancher), Luana Anders (Rancher's wife)
Arthur Penn's savage western starred Jack Nicholson as Tom
Logan, leader of a gang of cattle rustlers in Montana. Wealthy
rancher David Braxton (John McLiam) is determined to get
rid of them and hires Robert Lee Clayton (Brando), a
professional killer known as a Regulator, to do the job. As
Clayton isolates and kills the gang members one by one, he is
left at the end of the film with only Tom Logan to dispose of.
The two meet, silently, at a tiny mountain campsite at dawn.
Only one of them leaves. Brando had accepted the role of the
bounty hunter to bring in more money for his pet Indian
cause, but the film unfortunately had little commercial
success. "A pair of million dollar babies in a five-and-ten-cent
flick" was the verdict from Charles Champlin, critic of the Los
Angeles Times.

SUPERMAN — THE MOVIE (GB 1978)
Prod/Pierre Spengler. Dir/Richard Donner. Scr/Mario Puzo,
David Newman, Leslie Newman, Robert Benton. Music/
John Williams. Ph/Geoffrey Unsworth. Technicolor. GB
distribution/Columbia-EMI-Warner (Warner). Certificate
A. 143 mins.
With: Christopher Reeve (Clark Kent), Margot Kidder (Lois
Lane), Gene Hackman (Lex Luthor), Marlon Brando (Jor-
El), Susannah York (Lara), Marc McClure (Jimmy Olson),
Valerie Perrine (Eve Teschmacher), Ned Beatty (Otis),
Jackie Cooper (Perry White), Glenn Ford (Pa Kent), Phyllis
Thaxter (Ma Kent), Terence Stamp (General Zod), Sarah
Douglas (Ursa), Trevor Howard (1st Elder), Harry Andrews
(2nd Elder)
With some dazzling special effects work this epic production
is a re-telling of the Superman legend in which Jor-El
(Brando), senior-scientist-citizen of the planet Krypton,
saves his only son from the planet's imminent destruction by
sending him to Earth to grow up among alien people. By the
day he assumes the guise of newspaperman Clark Kent, but
uses his supernatural powers to fight for "truth, justice and
the American way". Whatever the morality of the fee Brando
received (he raked in $3 million for a ten-minute performance
and later sued the producers over his gross percentage), the
investment was worthwhile in terms of the stature he brought
not only to his part, but to the film as a whole.

APOCALYPSE NOW (US 1979)

Prod-dir/Francis Coppola. Scr/John Milius, Francis Coppola. Based on the novel "Hearts of Darkness" by Joseph Conrad. Music/Carmine Coppola, Francis Coppola. Ph/Vittorio Storara. Technicolor. GB distribution/Columbia-EMI-Warner. Certificate X. 153 mins.

With: Marlon Brando (Colonel Walter E Kurtz), Robert Duvall (Lt Colonel Bill Kilgore), Martin Sheen (Captain Benjamin L Willard), Frederic Forrest (Chef), Albert Hall (Chief), Sam Bottoms (Lance), Dennis Hopper (photo-journalist), Harrison Ford (Colonel Lucas), Larry Fishburne (Clean), G D Spradlin (General Corman)

Four years in the making, this was the trouble-plagued film that almost crippled Francis Coppola — emotionally and financially (the budget rose from $12 million to finally over $30 million). In Vietnam, Captain Willard (Martin Shaw) is sent on a mission up river to relieve the command of Colonel Kurtz (Brando), an officer who has gone berserk and is waging genocide in the Cambodian jungle. With some unforgettable images, and set-pieces of truly psychedelic horror, Coppola's staggering work gives a vision of war and madness that is powerful and manic. Although Brando only appeared in the last fifteen minutes, he was used brilliantly by the director to shift the film's emphasis away from visual spectacle to literary allusion.

THE FORMULA (US 1980)

Prod/Steve Shagan. Dir/John G Avildsen. Scr/Steve Shagan, based on his own novel. Music/Bill Conti. Ph/James Crabe. Metrocolor. GB distribution/CIC. Certificate AA. 117 mins.

With: George C Scott (Lieutentant Barney Caine), Marlon Brando (Adam Steiffel), Marthe Keller (Lisa), John Gielgud (Dr Abraham Esau), G D Spradlin (Clements), Beatrice Straight (Kay Neeley)

Los Angeles detective Barney Caine (George C Scott), investigating the murder of a police friend, stumbles on an international conspiracy to suppress a formula for synthetic fuel, developed by the Nazis during World War II. At the centre of the conspiracy is powerful oil magnate Adam Steiffel (Marlon Brando), knowing that if it becomes available, the formula will put him out of business. Unfortunately, the complicated storyline in this cynical, densely plotted thriller, was rendered all the more incomprehensible by Brando's inaudibility in some key scenes.

Opposite: in
The Formula